Table of Contents

Introduction

For at least two centuries, a fundamental tenet of American military theory is the idea that the function of military force is to serve a political purpose through strategy.[1] Operational art theory supports this idea by establishing the links between tactical actions and strategic objectives. Using operational art, the operational commander organizes his vision for the campaign into coherent actions informed by the purpose and understanding of strategic goals and policy objectives. Without the necessary link that operational art provides, tactical actions lack a unified purpose and can be counterproductive to the achievement of strategic goals. Using this premise, assuming the strategy is sound, one would expect a campaign conceived and executed within the guidelines of operational art to contribute to strategy aims.

Understanding and applying the art and science of operational art theory requires mastery achievable through a combination of rigorous study and experience. Historical case studies can provide concrete examples to test the validity of theory and doctrine. A critical analysis of the examples provided by history to "derive lessons that prove or negate the validity of operational [concepts] and ways of using one's military sources of power" is the best method of education available, short of real experience.[2] Thus, the thoughtful consideration of military history, as viewed through the perspective of theory and doctrine, is instructive for the military professional seeking to excel in both understanding and application of operational art.[3]

A historical example of both operational success and failure is the Korean War. America's full-scale involvement in the Korean War began on 25 June 1950, when the North

---

[1] Carl Von Clausewitz, *On War*, ed. Michael Howard, and Peter Paret (Princeton: Princeton University Press, 1984), 90-99.

[2] Milan Vego, "Military History and the Study of Operational Art," *JFQ: Joint Force Quarterly*, Number 57 (2010): 124-129.

[3] Clausewitz, *On War*, 170-174. Clausewitz discusses the necessity and limitations of historical examples in the study of warfare.

Korean People's Army (NKPA) invaded the south with 10 army divisions intent on reunifying the country through force of arms. In little more than a month, aided by the element of surprise and superiority in almost every category of military performance, the NKPA captured nearly ninety percent of the Korean Peninsula. The United States decided to intervene in the defense of the South and proceeded to press the United Nations (U.N.) for a resolution condemning the NKPA invasion. Days later, the U.N. passed a resolution calling upon member countries to render assistance to South Korea. General Douglas MacArthur, then in charge of U.S. forces in the Pacific and of the occupation of Japan, became Commander of the United Nations Forces. As U.N. and American forces echeloned into the fray, South Korea held on to the 160-mile Pusan Perimeter protecting the only viable seaport in South Korea at Pusan.

In the first year of the war, operations shifted the balance of advantage several times. The volatile character of the conflict demonstrated "rapid [changes in policy] with the success of the initial North Korean advance, then the equally dramatic U.N. counter-attack and eclipse of the North Koreans, followed by the intervention of China and the forcing back of U.N. forces, and finally the relative stabilization of the military conduct of war..."[4]

Several aspects of the Korean War remain relevant to operational art in contemporary conflicts. It had a complex and evolving strategy, a dramatic interplay of tactical success and failures, uncertainty and miscalculation, shortages of means to accomplish ends, and the difficult challenge to set the conditions for a satisfactory conclusion to the conflict.

An examination of three distinct operational periods in the Korean War using the requirements of operational art as described in the *Army Doctrinal Publication 3-0 Unified Land Operations* will reveal whether operational art was a factor in success or failure. The periods of the Korean War presented here are 1.) The U.N. Counter Offensive: Operation CHROMITE, 15

---

[4] Peter Lowe, *The Origins of the Korean War* (London: New York: Longman, 1955), 206.

Sept - 2 Nov 1950, 2.) The U.N. attack into North Korea triggering the Communist Chinese

Forces (CCF) intervention, 3 Nov 1950-24 Jan 1951, and 3.) U.N. Counteroffensive, 25 January-

8 July 1951.

This monograph argues that the commander met the requirements for operational art in

the first and third case, but not the second. Consequently, operations in the first and third case

correspond with operational success, in that they contributed to the strategic aim; however, the

second case was an operational failure. By examining the events of the Korean War using the

requirements of operational art found in doctrine, this monograph demonstrates when the

commander's campaign met the requirements of operational art and when it did not. Additionally,

this monograph will show that fulfilling the requirements of operational art is a prerequisite for

success in the pursuit of strategic objectives.

Despite the claim by many that it is "The Forgotten War," ample material exists for

research on the Korean War. Detailed historical accounts of the tactical actions of the Korean

War are easy to obtain, as are explanations of strategy. However, finding overt references or

analysis of operational art concepts in the Korean War is a difficult task. Considering the milieu

of the Korean War, this is understandable; operational art concepts first appeared in American

military doctrine in the 1980s. Thus, it is largely up to the researcher to establish the links

between the descriptions of tactical actions to the commander's achievement of strategic

objectives.

Of the numerous historical publications concerning the Korean War, these works

primarily fall into three broad areas of scholarship: the American strategy concerning Korea and

the Cold War, chronological and encyclopedic histories of the war itself, and tactical accounts of

the battles and fighting during the Korean War.

Several comprehensive works exist on the Korean War and they contributed to the

research in this monograph. Of the many books consulted, the best comprehensive accounts

include Allen Millet's first two volumes of a three volume set *The War for Korea , 1945-1950 A*

3

House Burning and *1950-1951 They Came From the North*, Roy Appleman's *South to the Naktong North to the Yalu*, and Clay Blair's *The Forgotten War: America and Korea in 1950-1953*. These books contain detailed accountings of the strategic context as well as detailed narratives of the tactics and operations. Each work contains a slightly different analysis of specific events, but all are factually consistent. Diverse interpretations of events from multiple sources provide the reader with a broader understanding of the complexities of the conflict. Two other books of honorable mention are General Matthew Ridgway's *The Korean War* and Max Hastings' *The Korean War*. Both offer insightful analysis of the political environment, strategy decisions, and the realities on the ground.

The U.S. Army's official history of the Korean War, which includes *South to the Naktong North to the Yalu*, is a four-volume collection. Each volume is a well-researched and detailed account covering the different periods of the war. In this collection, Billy Mossman's *The U.S. Army in the Korean War: Ebb and Flow November 1950-July 1951* and *Policy and Direction: The First Year* by James F. Schnabel are indispensable resources for military-focused research.

Several books explain specific aspects of the conflict. For example, Malcolm Cagle and Frank Mason's *The Sea War in Korea* describe naval operations. This book explains how the U.S. Navy achieved maritime superiority of the waters around Korea allowing U.N. forces to stop the communist invasion. Similarly, Robert Futrell's *The United States Air Force in Korea, 1950-1953* is a good analysis of aviation operations in Korea. Futrell provides an account of the Air Force's role in Korea providing transportation, evacuation, intelligence, and interdiction of enemy forces.

Roy Appleman is arguably the most prolific writer on the subject of the Korean War. In addition to *South to the Naktong North to the Yalu*, the research for this monograph relied on four of his other works. The first, *Disaster in Korea: The Chinese Confront MacArthur*, explains the Eighth Army's defeat in North Korea. The second, *East of Chosen: Entrapment and Breakout in Korea 1950* is primarily about the Marines but deals with command of X Corps and Eighth

Army. The third, *Escaping the Trap: U.S. Army X Corps in Northeast Korea 1950* is an inclusive study of the overall X Corps actions in North Korea. Finally, *Ridgway Duals for Korea* describes how General Matthew Ridgway consolidated and reinvigorated the Eighth Army and led them to regain the initiative, recapturing Seoul, and reestablishing the 38th parallel.

Operational Art: Doctrine, Definition, and Requirements

An analysis of operational art requires beginning with a common understanding and a definition. As is the case with all theory, operational art is an abstract concept. Doctrine, as an interpretation of theory, allows room for judgment.[5] The interpretation of operational art differs somewhat between joint and service doctrine. There is no right or wrong doctrinal interpretation of theory so long as the concepts convey a shared understanding. With this in mind, the next requirement is to choose which doctrinal reference to use for case analysis of this monograph.

The capstone publication establishing the doctrinal foundation of operational art for the U.S. Army is Army Doctrinal Publication 3-0 *Unified Land Operations* (ADP 3-0). ADP 3-0 provides a clear and succinct definition of operational art: "Operational art is the pursuit of strategic objectives, in whole or in part, through the arrangement of tactical actions in time, space, and purpose."[6] The core logic of operational art is that military force exists solely to contribute to the realization of strategic objectives. Embedded in this logic is a responsibility of political and senior military leaders to provide strategic guidance and the means to achieve it.

The function of operational art is to cognitively link tactical actions to strategic objectives. This requires the commander to visualize tactical actions and anticipate how they

---

[5] U.S. Department of the Army, *FM 1-02 2004: Operational Terms and Graphics* (Washington, D.C.: U.S. Department of the Army, 2004), 494. *FM 1-02* provides a definition of doctrine as: Fundamental principles by which the military forces or elements thereof guide their actions in support of national objectives. It is authoritative but requires judgment in application.

[6] U.S. Department of the Army, *ADP 3-0: Unified Land Operations* (October 2011), 9.

contribute to the strategic aim within the context of the operational environment. In other words, arrange tactical actions in time, space, and purpose. ADP 3-0 further elaborates:

> Hypothetically, military forces might accomplish a strategic objective through a single tactical action, eliminating the need for operational art. In reality, the scale of most modern conflicts and the ability of enemy forces to retain their operational capacity – even in the face of significant tactical defeats – make this an exceptionally rare event. Creating the military conditions necessary for the termination of conflict on favorable terms usually requires many tactical actions. The effective arrangement of military conditions in time, space, and purpose is the task of operational art.[7]

The task of this monograph is to assess if operational art concepts contributed to strategic success or failure in the Korean War. Did operational commanders cognitively link actions in time, space, and purpose in pursuit of the strategic objectives? To assist in this task, this monograph will primarily assess the included case studies using the requirements for operational art. ADP 3-0 describes the essential requirements for operational art:

> Operational art is how commanders balance risk and opportunity to create and maintain the conditions necessary to seize, retain, and exploit the initiative and gain a position of relative advantage while linking tactical actions to reach a strategic objective. It requires commanders who understand their operational environment, the strategic objectives, and the capabilities of all elements of their force. These commanders continually seek to expand and refine their Understanding and are not bound by preconceived notions of solutions.[8]

The above paragraph, describes six requirements for the commander to achieve in the application of operational art. They are:

1. Balance risk and opportunity.

2. Create and maintain the conditions necessary to seize, retain, and exploit the initiative.

3. Gain a position of relative advantage while linking tactical actions to reach a strategic objective.

---

[7] *Ibid.*, 9.

[8] *Ibid.*, 2.

4. Understand the operational environment, the strategic objectives, and the capabilities of all elements of the friendly force.

5. Continually seek to expand and refine understanding.

6. Avoid the constraint of preconceived notions of solutions.

This monograph examines whether operational commanders met the requirements of operational art during the three periods described above, and if operational art contributed to success. It attempts to prove that if a commander meets only some or none of these requirements, he likely will direct an ineffective campaign that does not achieve the political goal.

Strategic Context

Any critical analysis of operational art in a historical case requires an understanding of the strategic context. The Korean War is no exception. General Matthew B. Ridgway begins his book *The Korean War* by stating, "no one can fully understand the Korean War who does not own at least elemental knowledge of the geography, the history, the climate, and the economic lot of that country and its people. Knowledge of the strategic context of the Korean War enables the reader to better understand decisions made in the strategic, operational, and tactical dimensions, the motivations and decisions of the commanders, and how the U.S. led forces fought on the ground, in the air, and on the seas surrounding the Korean Peninsula."[9]

Doctrine provides a useful framework to outline the strategic context. *ADP 3-0* describes the strategic context defined by "the specific operational environment, the character of the friendly force, and the character of the threat."[10] The operational environment is a "composite of the conditions, circumstances, and influences that affect the employment of capabilities and bear

---

[9] Matthew B. Ridgway, *The Korean War* (Garden City, N.Y.: Doubleday, 1967), 1.

[10] U.S. Department of the Army, *ADP 3-0: Unified Land Operations* (October 2011), 9.

on the decisions of the commander."[11] The Korean War's operational environment was a dynamic mix of complexities "…greatly influenced by domestic conditions rooted deep in the history of Korea, and by the topography of the peninsula where it took place."[12] The war was also an event characterized by the power politics of stronger nations involving mainly the U.S., China, and the U.S.S.R., and the post World War II division of Korea into separate nations with conflicting ideologies.

Korea's geographic location makes it strategically important. Korea lies at the point "where the Russian, Chinese, and Japanese spheres meet – the apex of the three great power triangles in Asia."[13] Competing interests continued to shape the Korean War as China, the United States, and to a lesser extent, the U.S.S.R. sought to maintain Korea as a buffer against potential future aggression and protect national interests in the region.

The topography of Korea presented significant operational challenges. "Few habitable areas of the earth are more unsuited for large scale, modern military operations. The rugged landscape, a lack of adequate roads, rail lines and military harbors, the narrow peninsula, and, not least climatic extremes restrict and hamper maneuver, severely limit logistics support, and intensify the normal hardships of war."[14] Mountain ranges cover a majority of the Korean Peninsula, particularly in the North and East. The Taebaek Mountain Range separates the east and west coast with only one road in the north leading from Wonsan to Pyongyang. In 1950, few improved roads existed in Korea. The limited roads were crucial for the movement of supplies,

---

[11] *Ibid.*, 2.

[12] James F. Schnabel, *The United States Army and the Korean War: Policy and Direction: The First Year* (Washington, D.C.: U.S. Army Center of Military History, 1992), 1.

[13] Roy Edgar Appleman, *South to the Naktong, North to the Yalu* (Washington, D.C.: Department of the Army, 1961), 1.

[14] Schnabel, *The United States Army and the Korean War: Policy and Direction: The First Year,* 1.

and forces, particularly when fighting damaged or destroyed the rail network.[15] Overall, U.S. air superiority turned this into somewhat of an advantage as allied power punished the enemy using the roads, forcing the enemy to move at night and through the slower restrictive terrain. The effectiveness of close air support and air shaping operations was instrumental in supporting friendly maneuver.

Compounding movement constraints were the several major rivers and large streams flowing westward to the Yellow Sea and south to the Korea Strait.[16] These rivers and the few bridges that span them presented significant mobility considerations for military forces transiting north or south. Both sides attempted to use geography of Korea to their advantage during the course of the war.

Natural water boundaries surround Korea on all sides.[17] As a Peninsula, Korea has nearly 5,000 miles of coastline, with transportation routes following the coast. Few adequate harbors or ports existed on the peninsula. Extreme tidal variations occur on the west coast. This geographic reality made the peninsula exceptionally vulnerable to naval interdiction and blockade.[18] As a maritime power, the U.S. leveraged particular advantage in naval superiority during the course of the war for operational maneuver, logistics, and naval fires and air support.

Perhaps the most challenging aspect of the Korean geography was the effect of weather on men, equipment, and operations. The climate of the Korean peninsula differs dramatically from north to south and season to season. The southern regions experience warm weather affected

---

[15] David Halberstam, *The Coldest Winter: America and the Korean War* (New York: Hyperion, 2007), 507.

[16] South Korea's four largest waterways, the Han, Kum, Naktong, and Somjin Rivers descend from the Taebaek Mountains to the west and south. Both sides of the conflict used these natural defensive boundaries and the bridges that span them to their advantage.

[17] The Korean Peninsula's borders are defined by the Yellow sea on the west, the Sea of Japan on the East, the Korea Strait in the south, and the Yalu and Tumen Rivers on the north.

[18] Harry G. Summers, *Korean War Almanac* (New York: Facts on File, 1990), 4.

by warm ocean waters and the northern regions experience an extreme cold climate. The entire peninsula experiences the East Asian monsoon in midsummer, turning roads into muddy tracks and making off road movement impossible. The extreme cold in northern Korea, reaching -30 to -40 degrees, severely restricted operations. More than just a tactical consideration, weather also affected the conduct of operations.[19] Korea's extreme weather often hampered crucial air and naval operations. The onset of the severe weather conditions in North Korea contributed to MacArthur's decision to rush the rapid offensive into North Korea.

A prominent influence on the operational environment was the politics and history behind the decision to divide Korea at the 38th Parallel. At the end of World War II, world powers seeking to dismantle the Japanese Imperial Empire did not recognize Japanese dominion over Korea. There was general agreement that Korea was not yet capable of exercising and maintaining an independent government and a post war occupation was necessary as a temporary expedient.[20] In February 1945, the Yalta Conference granted to the Soviet Union European buffer zones – "satellite states accountable to Moscow"– as well as an expected Soviet pre-eminence in China and Manchuria in return for joining the Allied Pacific War effort against Japan.[21] If the Soviet Union would enter the war with Japan, it stood to gain significant territory and influence in the Asia Pacific Region, including sharing occupation of postwar Korea.

As per a U.S. – Soviet agreement, the U.S.S.R. declared war against Japan on 8 August 1945. The U.S. dropped nuclear weapons on the city of Hiroshima on 6 August 1945 and over Nagasaki on 9 August. On 15 August, six days after the bombing of Nagasaki, Japan

---

[19] Stanley Weintraub, *MacArthur's War: Korea and the Undoing of an American Hero* (New York: Free Press 2000), 167.

[20] James L. Stokesbury, *A Short History of the Korean War* (New York: W. Morrow 1988), 24. At the Cairo Conference in November 1943, Nationalist China, the United Kingdom, and the United States declared, "in due course Korea shall become free and independent."

[21] Joseph C. Goulden, *Korea: The Untold Story of the War* (New York: Times Books 1982),16-18.

announced its surrender to the Allies. The Soviet Red Army moved to occupy the northern part of the Korean peninsula as agreed. On 26 August, the Soviets halted at the 38th parallel for three weeks to await the arrival of U.S. forces in the south.[22]

U.S. military planners recommended the division of the Korean peninsula at the 38th parallel.[23] Despite popular belief, the location of the division was not arbitrary. They wanted to include Seoul and a minimum of two ports in the U.S. Korean Zone of Occupation.[24] The Soviets agreed to and abided by the proposed US occupation zone and the 38th parallel despite reaching the boundary almost a month before US forces arrived.

Most Koreans did not welcome either the trusteeship or occupation of foreign troops. After World War II, Koreans naturally identified with a broader global decolonization movement and the desire among the Korean people to be an independent and unified nation fueled strong nationalism.[25] Despite thirty-five years of Japanese occupation and subjugation, Koreans retained a distinct culture and national identity. Two separate views of nationalism, one communist and the other democratic emerged after World War II and formed the basis of the conflict between the divided Koreas. In 1948, the U.N. administered democratic elections for the government south of the 38th parallel, while the communist government in the North did not recognize them. Consequently, the U.N. declared the 38th parallel an internationally recognized boundary between North and South.[26]

---

[22] Summers, *Korean War Almanac*, 11.

[23] Allan R. Millett, *The War For Korea, 1945-1950: A House Burning* (Lawrence, KS: University Press of Kansas, 2005), 45.

[24] Goulden, *Korea: The Untold Story of the War*, 19.

[25] Millett, *The War For Korea, 1945-1950: A House Burning*, 12-13.

[26] Allan Reed Millett, *The War for Korea,1950-1951: They Came From the North* (Lawrence, KS: University Press of Kansas, 2005),125.

11

Tensions heightened between the Koreas as leaders in the North and South, created and propped up by their respective foreign backers, sought to unify the peninsula under their rule. Border clashes occurred frequently in the interwar period, and the two sides continued to grow increasingly entrenched in separate visions of a Unified Korea. In the north, the Soviets and Chinese aided North Korea's leader, Kim Il-Sung in a significant build-up of military capabilities. The U.S. assisted build-up of South Korea was considerably less robust. It provided the South Korean leader, Syngman Rhee, enough for defense but not enough to precipitate South Korean offensive actions to unify Korea.[27]

Adding to the tension in the region, the Chinese Communists won the nation's Civil War. In July 1949, the Chinese Communist Party established the People's Republic of China.[28] The perception of the growing communist threat was " a critical force in United States Policy toward the far east by the summer of 1950... the deep bitterness and frustration of the American people about the "loss" of China to the communists... merely persuaded much if the United States that anti-Communist regimes must be sustained and supported."[29] In the "logic and language" US policy makers, thwarting communist expansion would prevent a direct confrontation with the U.S.S.R. and an eventual third world war.[30] Following this logic led President Truman and the U.S. to commit to Korea in 1950.[31]

In January 1950, Secretary of State Dean G. Acheson publicly declared South Korea, Taiwan (Formosa) and Southeast Asia beyond the 'defense perimeter' of areas vital to American national interests and announced the withdrawal plan of U.S. forces from their World War II

---

[27] Max Hastings, *The Korean War* (New York: Simon and Schuster 1987), 391.

[28] Bevin Alexander, *Korea: The First War We Lost* (New York: Hippocrene 1986), 558.

[29] Hastings, *The Korean War*, 53.

[30] Michael D. Pearlman, *Truman & MacArthur: Policy, Politics, and the Hunger for Honor and Renown* (Bloomington: Indiana University Press, 2008), 30.

[31] *Ibid.,* 30.

security zones.[32] In doing so, he unintentionally signaled that the United States would not interfere with an invasion of South Korea. Russia's Stalin and China's Mao gave Kim cautious approval for an invasion of the South.[33]

The NKPA launched the invasion into the Republic of Korea with 135,000 men including eight infantry divisions, a tank brigade, three reserve divisions and five constabulary divisions.[34] Despite a multitude of signs and warnings, the NKPA invasion caught both the Republic of South Korea and the United States off-guard. The ROK could not react quickly enough with their eight ROK Army (ROKA) divisions to the surprise and shock effect the NKPA forces achieved.[35]

On 27 June, under the leadership and prompting of the United States, the U.N. condemned the invasion.[36] Armed with the Security Council's endorsement, President Truman took resolute action. He immediately authorized air and naval operations south of the 38th parallel to support ROK Forces. He ordered the U.S. Army to fight in Korea, directed the navy to shell North Korean targets ashore, authorized air strikes north of the 38th parallel, and reactivated the draft.[37]

On 7 July 1950, the Security Council passed a third resolution authorizing the United States to act as executive agent for the prosecution of the Korean War.[38] Truman immediately appointed General Douglas MacArthur the commander-in-chief of the United Nations Command,

---

[32] Goulden, *Korea: The Untold Story of the War*, 30.

[33] Millett, *The War for Korea, 1950-1951: They Came From the North*, 12.

[34] Summers, *Korean War Almanac*, 17.

[35] Millett, *The War for Korea, 1950-1951: They Came From the North*, 37,125.

[36] Robert Frank Futrell, *The United States Air Force in Korea, 1950-1953* (New York: Duell, Sloan and Pearce, 1961), 774.

[37] Bevin Alexander, *Korea: The First War We Lost* (New York: Hippocrene 1986), 33-34, 49-50.

[38] William Stueck, *The Korean War in World History* (Lexington, KY: The University Press of Kentucky, 2004), 58.

a coalition dominated by the United States, the Republic of Korea, Britain, Australia, New Zealand, and Canada.

General MacArthur was convinced that the ROKA "would soon be incapable of sustained resistance" and could not prevent the NKPA from seizing the entire peninsula.[39] The ROK Army lost 60 to 70 percent of its fighting strength in the first week and faced annihilation at the hands of the North Koreans.[40] General MacArthur requested the introduction of ground forces and promptly began committing elements of the four U.S. divisions in Japan to the fighting in Korea. On 5 July 1950, the first element of the Eighth U.S. Army in Japan engaged the North Koreans in South Korea. America optimistically thought U.S. presence and resolve to defend South Korea would deter the NKPA. However, U.S. presence did not result in this effect.[41]

Throughout July and August, Eighth Army and the ROKA, assisted by air and naval support, delayed NKPA units in a withdrawal south to Pusan. MacArthur correctly identified the port city of Pusan as the critical geographical point and resolved to defend it. In American hands, Pusan would be the strategic funnel through which the allied build-up of men and materiel would flow from shipment points in nearby Japan. If U.N. forces lost Pusan, they would lose the peninsula and the war. Return would be extremely difficult or impossible. MacArthur placed the U.S. Eighth Army in a cordon north and west of the city with orders to hold at all costs. The so-called 'Pusan Perimeter' encircled an area 50 miles wide and 80 miles in length.[42] The NKPA continued to launch attacks against the perimeter, but increasingly resupplied and reinforced

---

[39] Alexander, *Korea: The First War We Lost,* 19.

[40] Hastings, *The Korean War*, 391.

[41] Clay Blair, *The Forgotten War: America in Korea, 1950-1953* (New York: Anchor Books 1989), 94-99

[42] Appleman, *South to the Naktong, North to the Yalu*, 252-253

American and South Korean defenders held. In failing to pierce the perimeter the North Koreans lost the hope of a quick victory.

From the late 1940s to the early 1990s, the United States was engaged in a continuing state of political and military tension against communist countries often referred to as the Cold War. As the free world's only superpower, the United States accepted responsibility for "organizing the defense of the noncommunist world".[43] The U.S. strategic objective to defend South Korea was more than a U.N. restoration of the 38th parallel; it was a demonstration to the Soviet Union that the United States and the free world would not tolerate communist aggression.[44] Consequently, The United States viewed the conflict in Korea as a requirement to contain communist expansion in the Cold War.

Within the U.S. policy of containing communist expansion, the strategic objective was the preservation of the Republic of Korea and the restoration of the 38th Parallel. MacArthur's operational end state was the destruction of the NKPA. How far he could go to achieve this end was a matter of some debate. U.S. policy makers had justifiable concerns over Chinese and Soviet reaction to the unification of Korea under the U.N. banner. President Truman and the JCS viewed the Soviets as the real enemy as wanted to avoid escalation of the war into a global conflagration.[45] However, as early as 13 July 1950, MacArthur developed his plan to do more than reestablish the territorial integrity of the ROK. MacArthur's logic was with the destruction of the NKPA, the path to the unification of Korea would be wide open. Here is where U.S. Strategy failed to give clear guidance to its operational commander with a definitive long-range policy concerning the Korean War. MacArthur "disagreed with a Europe-first strategy and, as a

---

[43] Henry Kissinger, *Diplomacy* (New York: Simon & Schuster, 1994), 23.

[44] Callum A. MacDonald, *Korea: The War Before Vietnam* (New York: The Free Press,1985), 4.

[45] Pearlman, *Truman & MacArthur: Policy, Politics, and the Hunger For Honor and Renown*, 139.

result, cared little about preventing the Korean conflict either from expanding into other areas or from involving directly Communist China, the Soviet Union, or both. The idea of halting U.S. ground forces in Korea at the 38th parallel so as to avert Soviet or Chinese intervention never occurred to him."[46] MacArthur was willing "...to carry the war as far as the Kremlin if necessary."[47] Clay Blair in his book *The Forgotten War*, effectively summarizes MacArthur's campaign plan:

> He would first "isolate the battlefield" by closing off NKPA supply routes at the China and Russia borders with American air power . . . After the battlefield had been isolated and stabilized MacArthur went on, his intention was not merely to drive the NKPA back across the 38th Parallel but rather to "destroy" it. This he would do by reviving the recently canceled Inchon amphibious landing plan, designed to trap the NKPA in giant pincers between those forces and an attacking Eighth Army . . . After the NKPA had been destroyed the problem would be to "compose and Unite Korea," and that might require American occupation of the entire peninsula.[48]

General MacArthur, as the unified commander was designated Commander in Chief, Far East. He received orders directly from the Joint Chiefs of Staff and the Army Chief of Staff. The Army Component Command for Korea was Lieutenant General Walton H. Walker's Eighth U.S. Army. In June of 1950, Eighth Army consisted of four under-strength divisions (1st Cavalry and 7th, 24th, and 25th Infantry Divisions). Other units that would eventually deploy to Korea by the end of September were the 1st Marine Division, and the 2d Infantry Division. During the first six months, MacArthur established X Corps, which combined the 1st Marine Division, the 7th Infantry Division and other US Army and ROKA units under its command. In February 1951, MacArthur placed X Corps and its units under the command of Eight Army. The only American

---

[46] Stueck, *The Korean War in World History*, 75.

[47] Edwin P. Hoyt, *On To the Yalu* (New York: Stein and Day, 1985), 194.

[48] Blair, *The Forgotten War: America in Korea, 1950-1953*, 124.

soldiers stationed in Korea at the start of the war were the 468 members of the United States Military Advisory Group to the Republic of Korea (KMAG).[49]

The status of U.S. ground forces at the time of the North Korean invasion was not favorable for the defense of Korea. Forces in the Far East were postured to defend the Japanese islands from soviet invasion, however an unlikely scenario, but not much else. Defensive plans for Korea did not exist. By 1949, all U.S. occupation forces redeployed from Korea and only a handful of KMAG advisors to the ROKA remained in Korea. Government economies in the aftermath of WWII reduced the U.S. Army active strength to approximately 591,000, about on third of which were serving overseas in occupation duties. Lack of funds and occupation duties hampered training programs. Additionally, post war reductions cut supply and procurement to the very basics, exacerbating the readiness problems.[50]

One of MacArthur's primary objectives was keeping the traumatized ROKA fighting. U.S. assistance to the ROKA deliberately created a forced "organized entirely for defense…unable to take an offensive war across the border."[51] On 15 June 1950, the Korean Army numbered 95,000.[52] The National Police, organized for internal security and anti-guerilla activity, totaled 48,273. The ROKA had eight divisions, four of which had only two regiments, and two separate regiments comprised the Korean Army organization. Four divisions and one regiment defended the 38th parallel; the remainder was in reserve. Yet, this force, which appeared formidable, was hardly prepared to fight in a sustained operation. They were ill equipped and marginally trained with only 10-15 days of supply.[53] The meager Korean logistical situation

---

[49] Millett, *The War for Korea, 1950-1951: They Came From the North,* 18.

[50] Alexander, *Korea: The First War We Lost,* 46-52.

[51] Brian Catchpole, *The Korean War, 1950-53* (New York: Carroll & Graf Publishers 2000), 9.

[52] Stokesbury, *A Short History of the Korean War,* 39-40.

[53] Millett, *The War for Korea,1950-1951: They Came From the North,* 29-31.

steadily deteriorated readiness. Supply and service provided logistic support only on a bare subsistence standard. Fifteen percent of the weapons and thirty-five percent of the vehicles of the Korean Army were unserviceable.[54]

The United States actively fought two enemies in the Korean War – North Korea and China. When the Korean War began, China was not involved. China issued an explicit warning they would intervene if United Nations forces crossed into North Korea. U.S. leaders ignored this warning. Chinese decided to enter the war in October 1950, when U.N. intervention caused the collapse of the NKPA and U.N forces crossed into the 38th parallel.[55] North Korea's strategic aim was the unification of Korea under the leadership of the North. The Chinese believed that the U.N. and a unified Korea posed a threat on their border and were afraid the United Nations would use the Korean War to reopen the Chinese Civil War whose outcome the United States had not yet accepted. The U.S.S.R. was at the time backing both countries with arms and support.[56] The Soviets saw the expansion of communism as directly beneficial to their national interests.

Unlike the military buildup in South Korea, the NKPA, aided by the Soviets, amassed an impressive force capable of offensive action. "By June of 1950, the North Koreans built up a formidable military force: 130, 000 men under arms, plus 100,000 trained reserves."[57] The Soviets provided the NKPA weapons, including 150 T-34 tanks and significant indirect fire capability including 122 mm howitzers, 45 mm antitank guns, and heavy and medium mortars.[58]

---

[54] *Ibid.,* 30.

[55] Roy Edgar Appleman, *Disaster in Korea: The Chinese Confront MacArthur* (College Station TX: Texas A & M University Press 1989), 10-11.

[56] Millett, *The War for Korea,1950-1951: They Came From the North,* 29, 292-293.

[57] E.B. Porter, *Sea Power: A Naval History,* 2nd ed. (Annapolis, MD: Naval Institute Press, 1981), 363.

[58] Schnabel, *The United States Army and the Korean War Policy and Direction: The First Year,* 39.

An additional factor that affected the character of the NKPA was the experience level and number of trained personnel. Approximately one third of NKPA personnel served in combat with Chinese Communist forces during World War II against the Japanese. After World War II, many continued to serve with the CCF against the Chinese Nationalist during the Chinese Civil War. After the Chinese Civil War, many battle-hardened and experienced soldiers repatriated to Korea and formed a substantial portion of the NKPA.[59]

North Korea began the war with 180 Russian built planes, but after the first weeks of the war, they were nearly all destroyed by U.N. air forces. U.N. air forces achieved air superiority after the first month of the war.[60] When China entered the war, they had a formidable air force of 650 planes. By the end of the war, the Communist Chinese Air Force (CCAF) increased to 1050 planes including 445 MiG-15 jets. [61] The CCAF primarily focused on defense against U.N. bombers and largely ignored aerial interdiction and close air support missions. The CCAF enjoyed a significant advantage of sanctuary in Manchuria, which was off limits to U.N. attack.[62]

Neither North Korea nor Chinese Communist naval forces posed a significant threat to the United Nations during the Korean War. While enemy naval forces were not a significant threat, the use of naval mines was damaging to the U.N. effort, particularly at the Wonsan Harbor. During the course of the war, mines sank five U.S. warships.[63]

Between 13 and 25 of October 1950, the CCF crossed into North Korea with a force of 380,000 men organized into two army groups. The two Army groups attacked U.N. forces in November 1950. The CCF lacked sufficient supporting arms. Their rifles consisted of "a mixture

---

[59] Millett, *The War for Korea,1950-1951: They Came From the North,* 8-9.

[60] Futrell, *The United States Air Force in Korea, 1950-1953*, 31-32.

[61] Summers, *Korean War Almanac*, 83.

[62] Stanlis David Milkowski, "After Inchon," in *On Operational Art,* ed. Clayton R. Newell and Michael D. Krause (Washington D.C.: U.S. Army Center of Military History, 1994) , 222.

[63] Summers, *Korean War Almanac*, 199.

of Chinese, Japanese, German, and Czech" weapons.[64] They lacked sustainment, particularly in food and ammunition.[65] CCF tactics were not sophisticated. Lacking supporting arms, the CCF used infiltration and massive frontal assaults aimed at fixing and isolating U.N. formations. Initially these tactics were very successful as the U.N. forces fought separated and not in a position to give mutual support. Later, when U.N. forces organized into prepared defensive positions offering mutual support and maximum use of supporting arms, CCF tactics resulted in massive casualties, and were not as successful.[66]

As both NKPA and later the Chinese operations extended further South, their material and reinforcements were increasingly vulnerable to attacks from allied air. MacArthur's campaign design isolated the battlefield and exploited the biggest weakness in the NKPA force, their inability to sustain operations with little or no logistics planning and preparation. The effect of NKPA extended lines of communication and bombing shaped MacArthur's chances for success in Korea.[67]

By the end of July 1950, the last of the retreating U.N. forces in Korea were south of the Naktong River, including the American 2nd division, 24th division, 25th division, 1st Calvary division, 1st Marine brigade, and five ROK divisions, consolidated in a defense known as the Pusan Perimeter.[68] For six weeks, U.N. forces fought desperately to retain the Pusan perimeter from successive attacks and counter attacks pushing the Eighth Army to exhaustion. Supplies and reinforcements continued to arrive by ship at Pusan. Until the perimeter stabilized, the U.N. strategic objective–defense of the ROK–remained uncertain.

---

[64] Appleman, *Disaster in Korea: The Chinese Confront MacArthur*, 456.

[65] *Ibid.,* 351.

[66] *Ibid.,* 353.

[67] Futrell, *The United States Air Force in Korea, 1950-1953*, 262-268.

[68] Hastings, *The Korean War*, 84-89.

Case One: Operation CHROMITE: 15 Sept - 2 Nov 1950

Operation CHROMITE began with the amphibious assault at Inchon on 15 September and subsequent breakout of the Pusan Perimeter by Eighth Army. It ended with the link up of forces south of the Han River and consolidation and the capture of Seoul. CHROMITE is an exceptional illustration of operational skill, fulfilling all the requirements of operational art. CHROMITE consisted of the following missions:

1. Seize the port of Inchon and capture a force beachhead line.
2. Advance and seize Kimpo airfield.
3. Cross the Han River.
4. Occupy blocking positions North, Northeast, and East of Seoul.
5. Using forces in the Inchon-Seoul area as an anvil crush the Communists with a stroke from the south by Eighth Army.

Through operational maneuver aimed at achieving surprise, U.N. forces limited their losses to 3,500 casualties – comparatively low to those that might have occurred from a frontal attack against the NKPA. General MacArthur's forces demoralized the NKPA, destroyed large amounts of equipment, killed 14,000 of its soldiers, and captured 7,000 enemy prisoners of war.[69]

Landing on 15 September 1950, the Marines took the fortress island of Wolmi-do and then captured Inchon. The 7th Infantry Division landed on the 17th of July and pushed on to join the Marines, in the attack to Seoul. Eighth Army broke free of the Pusan Perimeter, pushed the North Koreans back and eventually joined X Corps. U.N. forces recaptured Seoul on 29 September. In a special ceremony, General MacArthur returned the city to ROK president Syngman Rhee.

CHROMITE was a brilliant example of balancing risk and opportunity. X Corps, composed of 1ˢᵗ Marine Division and 7ᵗʰ Army Division landed on Korea's west coast, cutting off

---

[69] Appleman, *U.S. Army in the Korean War, South to the Naktong, North to the Yalu*, 489.

and entrapping the North Koreans besieging Pusan. Near simultaneously, Eighth Army conducted a breakout of the Pusan perimeter and defeated the NKPA between the pincers of the two forces.

Several aspects of the amphibious landing at Inchon were risky in themselves, but together, many assumed that the risk was unacceptable. The harbor on the west coast of Korea has an extreme tidal range, dangerous approaches, and a high seawall. The geography of the operation made the landing achievable only a handful of times a year, and then only brief windows of opportunity existed.[70] X Corps required the reassignment of the First Marine Provisional Brigade to 1st Marine Division from its critical support to the Pusan perimeter. Amphibious expertise of the staff, although residual in the higher ranks left over from World War II, was lacking in the lower ranks across the force. Just five years after World War II, demobilization of forces and equipment depleted the ranks and made amphibious operations almost unthinkable.[71]

What was once the greatest amphibious force in the world was now barely able to scrap together enough resources and trained personnel to conduct a two-division amphibious assault. MacArthur lacked enough amphibious ships to carry out the task, but salvaged an amphibious task force fleet from decommissioned ships crewed by former Japanese Navy personnel. However, the potential benefit of accepting risk is often greater opportunity. The biggest aspect mitigating MacArthur's risk was the potential for operational surprise. "MacArthur's selection of Inchon as the point of assault was a blend of his strategic, psychological, political, and military reasoning."[72]

---

[70] Robert D. Heinl, "Inchon, 1950," in *Assault from the Sea: Essays on the History of Amphibious Warfare* ed. Merrill L. Bartlett (Annapolis, MD: Naval Institute Press, 1983), 340.

[71] *Ibid.,* 340-343.

[72] Cagle and Manson, *The Sea War in Korea*, 77.

In this phase, MacArthur effectively created the conditions to seize the initiative from the enemy. In order to take back the initiative, Macarthur had to first build enough combat power to go on the offensive. MacArthur's preparation for CHROMITE began months earlier with shaping actions against the NKPA and efforts to build a force large enough to take the offensive. The U.N. employment of supporting arms was critical to gaining the initiative. As the North Koreans began attacking south, Truman authorized the use of air and naval assets in support of South Korean operations. Strategic and tactical bombing operations began to slow the progress and limit freedom of movement of the NKPA as the buildup of forces in Pusan began. He persuaded Washington to send forces to halt the NKPA offensive. Throughout the summer, the United States committed all the forces it could muster to delay the NKPA and defend the Pusan Perimeter. By August, the remnants of five ROKA divisions, four Army infantry divisions, a Marine Provisional Brigade, and a British Infantry brigade defended the 160-mile perimeter. Replacements and supporting units including artillery and tank battalions continued to flow in daily. By August, U.N. forces strength relative to the NKPA was almost 2:1 and was better armed and supplied.[73]

It is clear that MacArthur understood the operational environment, the strategic environment, and the capabilities of his force. His strategic objective was the preservation of the Republic of Korea under the political purpose of containing communist expansion. MacArthur's operational objective was destruction of the NKPA. To accomplish this end, CHROMITE leveraged an indirect approach to attack the enemy's key vulnerability – the lines of communication of the enemy. During the movement south, the enemy's lines of communication became increasingly spread-out and vulnerable. The deliberate defenses around the Pusan

---

[73] Hastings, *The Korean War,* 103. "…in reality. Kim Il Sung's ruined regiments besieging Pusan could now only muster some 70,000 men, against a total of 140,000 in Walker's command."

perimeter caused further vulnerabilities as the enemy's concentrations around Pusan made them open to air interdiction, and increased their necessity on supply through lines of communication. With the NKPA attack now stalled, maritime and air superiority established, and a strong force that in all areas was capable of domination of the NKPA, MacArthur was ready to seize initiative away from the enemy.

MacArthur recognized his force lacked sufficient amphibious capable forces in the Far East Command to execute such a bold maneuver under the precarious conditions at Inchon. He needed Navy and Marine Corps expertise. He requested the 1st Marine Division and assembled a planning staff. Both Navy and Marine planners, with experience from the World War II campaigns in the Pacific produced the detailed plan. To conduct the landing at Inchon and liberation of Seoul, the Navy created an expeditionary Task Force, Joint Task Force 7, and MacArthur established X Corps, consisting of the 1st Marine Division and the 7th Infantry Division.[74]

MacArthur's efforts to shape the operational environment allowed the U.N force to gain a position of relative advantage while linking tactical actions to reach a strategic objective. MacArthur effectively linked the shaping actions of the U.N. air and naval forces against the NKPA, and the Eighth Army to halt the NKPA advance and retain the port of Pusan, X Corps to conduct operational envelopment, and finally all the components of his force to liberate Seoul and defeat the NKPA. The persistent weakening of enemy supply, the continued build-up of friendly forces and logistics at the Pusan Perimeter, and dominance of the air and sea began to turn the tide on the war by giving U.N. forces a position of relative advantage. These actions also purchased crucial time to organize X Corps and conduct planning and preparations

---

[74] Heinl, "Inchon, 1950," in *Assault from the Sea: Essays on the History of Amphibious Warfare,* 453.

for CHROMITE. Through Operation CHROMITE, MacArthur further solidified his advantage through the seizing of Suwon and Kimpo airfields and the Inchon port, allowing him to rapidly flow supplies and troops to the front lines. Additionally, the recapture of Seoul gave the South Koreans and their armed forces renewed spirit to continue fighting in the war.[75]

Operation CHROMITE changed the entire course of the war and was a brilliant example of linking tactical actions in pursuit of strategic objectives. In a synchronized attack U.N. forces took advantage of space, time, and force, and employed operational intelligence, operational fires, and operational maneuver that allowed them to concentrate their forces against the NKPAs critical weaknesses and vulnerabilities. By liberating Seoul and dislocating the communist logistics system, CHROMITE caused the disintegration of the NKPA. The result of this phase of the war was the U.N. returned to the 38th Parallel and thus the Republic of Korea preserved.

MacArthur continually sought to expand and refine his understanding of the operational environment. During this phase of the war, MacArthur traveled frequently to the front lines of Korea to gain firsthand knowledge of the situation. He correctly assessed the NKPA was near culmination stemming from its long supply lines and massive casualties. NKPA casualties before the execution of CHROMITE depleted the ranks of the communists who lost almost 58, 000 troops and only had 40 of its original 150 T-34 tanks remaining. The NKPA overextended supply lines ran almost 300 miles from Pyongyang to the units scattered on a wide front.[76] MacArthur focused air and naval fires to further weaken the enemy's lines of communication and combat formations. They were under constant attack from naval fires and U.N. air support from carriers and bases in Japan. Although the defense of the Pusan perimeter was tenuous, MacArthur knew the well-supplied and well-supported troops could hold long

---

[75] D. Clayton James, *The Years of MacArthur: Triumph and Disaster 1945-1964,* Volume 3 (Boston: Houghton Mifflin 1985), 482-484.

[76] Blair, *The Forgotten War: America in Korea, 1950-1953,* 172.

enough to execute CHROMITE. All MacArthur felt needed to accommodate a breakout was to sever the vulnerable North Korean supply lines.

Despite serious problems with Inchon as a landing site, and opposition from the Joint Chiefs of Staff, MacArthur continued to plan for the landing at Inchon. Several of his staff as well as they JCS preferred a shorter, less risky envelopment.[77] However, MacArthur recognized that only Inchon would result in a deep enough envelopment to liberate Seoul and cut the NKPA supply lines. MacArthur correctly identified Seoul as the center of gravity for the enemy. Seoul was a point where major lines of communication from north to south converge, making it a strategic hub for logistics. Recapturing Seoul effectively unhinged the North Koreans and cut them off. Additionally, as the capitol of South Korea, its recapture had a major psychological effect.

During CHROMITE, preconceived notions of solutions did not constrain Macarthur, possibly because his plan worked so well. MacArthur was famous for his strong opinion, bordering on obstinacy and his ability to persuade others to his way of thinking. This does not detract from the fact that his assessment of the situation at the beginning of the conflict was sound, and his actions regarding Inchon as a landing site, the decisiveness of CHROMITE, and the ability to get the forces he required. Unfortunately, this is almost the last time he was right. Nevertheless, the conception of CHROMITE was both creative and original. The location of the landing and the status of his force made many aspects contentious but thorough planning and execution of Operation CHROMITE provided hope for the U.N. forces. For the first time during the Korean War, the U.N. forces achieved operational success against the NKPA. With CHROMITE, MacArthur achieved the principle of surprise, maneuvered his forces to put the

---

[77] Millet, *The War For Korea, 1950-1951: They Came from the North,* 214-215.

enemy in a position of disadvantage, seized and exploited the initiative, and allocated combat power to decisive points in the area of operations.

As planned, CHROMITE severed the North Korean overextended supply lines.[78] It effectively linked tactical actions in time, space and purpose and contributed to the strategy objective. U.N. forces soundly defeated the NKPA and forced them out of South Korea. As September ended, U.N. forces reached the 38th parallel and halted shortly. CHROMITE achieved the goals of the U.N. resolution; the border between South Korea and North Korea was reestablished. In CHROMITE, all the requirements of operation art as outlined in *ADP 3-0* were present in MacArthur's plan and the operational success is undeniable.

After the success of CHROMITE, MacArthur and the United States were more than willing to lead U.N. forces into a new phase of the war.[79] On 30 September, China stated it would not tolerate the invasion of North Korea. On 3 October, China stated that if U.N. forces entered North Korea, China would intervene. U.S. State Department officials discounted these warnings as empty threats. 320,000 Chinese staged in Manchuria. U.S. citizens thought the war would be over soon.

On 27 September, the same day MacArthur returned Seoul to South Korea, MacArthur received the mission from the Joint Chiefs of Staff to "destroy the North Korean Armed Forces and the authority to conduct military operations north of the 38th parallel to that end."[80]

---

[78] Stueck, *The Korean War in World History*, 88.

[79] James, *The Years of MacArthur: Triumph and Disaster 1945-1964*, 417-418.

[80] Milkowski, "After Inchon," in *On Operational Art*, 224.

Case Two: Attacking into North Korea and CCF Intervention, 1 Oct 1950-24 Jan 1951

The U.N. attack into North Korea can be considered a separate phase in the Korean War. This phase began in October of 1950 with the U.N. pursuit of the NPKA into North Korea, subsequent seizure of Pyongyang, and the drive to the Manchurian border on the Yalu River. It ended with the Chinese attack on U.N. forces, causing the U.N. withdrawal from Korea and the eventual recapture of Seoul by the Communists. In contrast to CHROMITE, the ill-conceived U.N. attack into North Korea was a hastily planned, unsynchronized episode with competing tactical actions that quickly unraveled U.N. momentum. It did not sufficiently achieve any of the six requirements of operational art.

Although CHROMITE achieved operational success, the hammer and anvil strategy envisioned for X Corps and Eighth Army was not completely effective. The linkup between Eighth Army and X Corps took over a week. As a result, an estimated 25,000 to 40,000 NKPA soldiers slipped north escaping U.N. forces.[81] North Korea's leader, Kim Il Sung did not offer to surrender and sufficient NKPA forces remained to pose a credible threat to the security of the Korean peninsula.

America now had to decide how to "relate its military objectives to its political goals" in choosing how to terminate the conflict.[82] "Truman had three choices; He could order a halt on the 38th parallel and restore the *status quo ante*. He could authorize an advance farther north to exact a penalty for aggression. He could authorize MacArthur to unify Korea up to the Chinese border; in other words, to let the outcome of the war be dictated entirely by military considerations."[83]

---

[81] Hoyt, *On To the Yalu*, 194.

[82] Kissinger, *Diplomacy*, 912.

[83] *Ibid.*, 480.

After the successful Inchon landing, American opinion favored the later course of action–U.N. forces should move into North Korea, liberate its population, and unite the country.[84] This course of action aligned well with the 1947 U.N. aim of a unified Korea with democratized processes.[85] Since Kim Il Sung refused to capitulate, authorizing MacArthur to conduct ground operations in North Korea was "justifiable."[86]

On 27 September, twelve days after the Inchon landing, MacArthur received authorization from the JCS to cross the 38th Parallel:

> Your military objective is the destruction of the North Korean Armed Forces. In attaining this objective you are authorized to conduct military operations...north of the 38th Parallel in Korea, provided that at the time of such operation there has been no entry into North Korea by major Soviet or Chinese Communist Forces, no announcement of intended entry, nor a threat to counter our operations militarily in North Korea... [87]

With JCS authorization, , U.S. and ROK forces attacked with orders not to cross into Manchuria or conduct aerial attacks north of the border. The ROKA continued the pursuit of the NKPA, attacking into North Korea on 2 October. The South Koreans conducted a relentless pursuit of the NKPA and seized Pyongyang on 11 October. On the same day, the ROK I Corps seized Wonsan before X Corps could complete its backload on amphibious shipping. Eighth Army, due to shortages in supply, did not commence drive towards Pyongyang until parallel 8-9 October. Nine days later X Corps completed its backload at Inchon. The X Corps plan called for the First Marine Division to seize a base of operations at Wonsan while 7th Division would attack west to link-up with Eighth Army near Pyongyang. [88]

---

[84] Stokesbury, *A Short History of the Korean War*, 276.

[85] Millett, *The War for Korea,1945-1950: A House Burning*, 121-122.

[86] Hastings, *The Korean War*, 391.

[87] Schnabel, *The United States Army and the Korean War Policy and Direction: The First Year*, 182.

[88] Milkowski, "After Inchon," in *On Operational Art*, 422-21.

In mid-October President Truman and General MacArthur conferred on Wake Island as U.N. troops reached the limit of advance prescribed in the JCS . In discussions with Truman on Wake Island, MacArthur told the president he did not think the Chinese would intervene to save North Korea. He further added, if the Chinese entered the war, he would be able to isolate them from Korea or defeat them in "the greatest slaughter."[89]

On 12-16 October, Chinese forces began crossing the border into North Korea undetected. As U.N. forces moved north, evidence of communist Chinese forces in Korea increased. Eighth Army forces continued their drive and secured Pyongyang by 21 October. On 24 October, General MacArthur unilaterally moved the limit of advance to the Manchurian border and ordered his forces to proceed with all available forces to the north border of Korea on the Yalu.[90] The Communist Chinese, concerned about American intentions, again warned of action if the advance continued. On 26 October, the first South Korean Units of ROK II Corps reached the Manchurian border on the Yalu River. Almost immediately, the CCF attacked and nearly destroyed two ROK divisions of ROK II Corps and the 1st Calvary Division, causing Walker to retreat to a defensive line south of the Chongchon River.[91] By the end of October, "the Chinese had destroyed four regiments of the ROK 6th and 8th divisions–the bulk of ROK II Corps–as effective fighting units."[92]

On 6 November, the CCF broke contact and withdrew. However , MacArthur, still convinced that the CCF threat was a bluff, remained confident that China would not enter the

----

[89] Schnabel, *The United States Army and the Korean War Policy and Direction: The First Year,* 213-14.

[90] Appleman, *U.S. Army in the Korean War, South to the Naktong, North to the Yalu,* 812.

[91] Appleman, *Disaster in Korea: The Chinese Confront MacArthur,* 456.

[92] *Ibid.,* 20.

war.[93] He ordered both Almond and Walker of to continue the advance north.[94] On 23 November, the main Chinese assault attacked U.N. forces causing them to withdraw under pressure toward both coasts to evacuate North Korea. X Corps evacuated at Hungnam and disembarked at Pusan. They immediately deployed back north to join Eighth Army into the fight. The CCF attack advanced and recaptured Seoul on 5 January.

The decision and the conduct of ground operations in North Korea demonstrate an unfortunate evaluation of risk in relation to opportunity. The opportunity to end the five-year division of Korea presented a tempting strategic opportunity with obvious benefits. However, attacking into North Korea carried an enormous risk of widening the war with China or the U.S.S.R., whose intentions were still unclear. The decision to conduct ground operations in North Korea was not MacArthur's decision alone, but it was the course he preferred. Before the CCF intervention, MacArthur was "…confident that the war for Korea had been won, and that his armies were victorious. Now it was just a matter of cleaning up."[95] Macarthur also remained convinced that the threat of Chinese intervention was a bluff, despite intelligence that the Chinese had massed 450,000 troops in Manchuria.

During this phase, MacArthur unnecessarily assumed considerable operational risk. The plan for operations in North Korea relied on the incorrect assumption that China or the U.S.S.R would not intervene. In the hasty reassessment of strategic objectives, little planning for operations after CHROMITE took place. MacArthur did not inform his subordinates of the plan for the Wonsan amphibious maneuver until 26 September.[96] In light of the complicated

---

[93] Blair, *The Forgotten War: America in Korea, 1950-1953*, 447-449.

[94] James, *The Years of MacArthur: Triumph and Disaster 1945-1964,* 527.

[95] Hastings, *The Korean War*, 391.

[96] Milkowski, "After Inchon," in *On Operational Art*, 422.

maneuver, the planning horizon was extremely short. Had subordinates known earlier, they could have postured resources and forces to mitigate the impacts.

U.N. forces lacked sufficient planning to counter CCF intervention as well. MacArthur and his subordinate leaders largely discounted the CCF threat. The only planned measure taken to counter the contingency was to isolate North Korea from Manchuria through air operations against enemy forces and bridges on the Yalu.[97] For various reasons, air operations were unsuccessful at preventing "men and material in large force from pouring across the bridges over the Yalu from Manchuria."[98] U.N. bombing was successful in destroying only 4 of the 12 main bridges spanning the Yalu.[99] Further, CCF forces and material continued to cross on pontoon bridges and across the frozen Yalu River ice. However, even if U.N. air forces had successfully isolated North Korea from Manchuria, "the bulk of the 300,000 CCF troops hiding in North Korea, had arrived there before the bridge raids were under way…"[100]

In neglecting to respect the potential and effect of CCF intervention, MacArthur assumed unnecessary operational risk and left himself and his command susceptible to operational surprise. MacArthur squandered the opportunity to exploit success and maintain the initiative with inadequate planning and anticipation of the transition to operations in North Korea and the potential for CCF intervention.

As he attacked into North Korea, MacArthur's plan failed to maintain and exploit the initiative gained at Inchon. Several events caused the initiative to pass to the enemy in this phase. First and most prominent was the failure to anticipate and plan for China's intervention and the CCF offensive. Without a plan, U.N. forces ceded the initiative to the enemy and, in

---

[97] Appleman, *Disaster in Korea: The Chinese Confront MacArthur*, 670.

[98] Futrell, *The United States Air Force in Korea, 1950-1953*, 222.

[99] James, *The Years of MacArthur: Triumph and Disaster 1945-1964*, 524.

[100] *Ibid.*, 524.

operational shock, hastily retreated out of North Korea. U.N. forces possessed several advantages in relation to the capabilities of the CCF. U.N. forces were "a modern force with the latest weapons and communications, transport and resupply system with naval and air supremacy."[101] In contrast, the CCF was "a primitive force of light infantry with only light hand weapons, for the most part, no resupply capability and primitive communications."[102] When Eighth Army conducted its precipitous withdrawal from North Korea, it represented "the total disintegration of the fighting force."[103] Eighth Army failed to conduct rear guard actions or attempt to maintain contact with CCF lead elements. This resulted in a complete lack of knowledge of the enemy's disposition, and unnecessary loss of life and equipment. U.N. forces had the capability to counter and defeat the Chinese attack in the North but leadership failed to develop a comprehensive plan for the CCF contingency and did not provide solid leadership when the CCF attacked.

Another event contributing to the loss of the initiative was the effect of the decision to use X Corps to conduct an amphibious envelopment. Dictated by the compartmented terrain and the need to secure a logistics port on the eastern side of the peninsula, MacArthur planned to land X Corps on the east coast at Wonsan. Additionally, X Corps would seal the Wonsan-Pyongyang corridor to trap fleeing NKPA forces. Securing the Port at Wonsan was a logistical necessity –the U.N. logistics system was in a precarious position with most supplies originating from Pusan over roads growing steadily worse with increased use. Six months of fighting heavily damaged the road and rail system in the entire country and Inchon could not supply forces on the east coast. However, The Wonsan operation did more to negatively affect the momentum of the U.N. attack than to positively influence it. The combination of the backload at Inchon, heavy mining at Wonsan Harbor, and travel time delayed the landing of X Corps for several weeks, effectively

---

[101] Appleman, *Disaster in Korea: The Chinese Confront MacArthur,* 353.

[102] *Ibid.*, 353.

[103] Halberstam, *The Coldest Winter: America and the Korean War*, 483.

33

taking X Corps out of the fight. Additionally, the backload of X Corps divisions at Inchon tied up the port and delayed the offload of critical supplies at both Wonsan and Pusan.

Because of the Wonsan move, Eighth Army suffered critical logistics shortfalls during its attack into North Korea.[104] Logistics delayed Eight Army's attack north by several days allowing NKPA remnants to reconstitute and defend the approaches to Pyongyang.[105] After months of fighting on the Pusan perimeter, and the rapid advance of the Pusan breakout to link up with X Corps at Seoul, Eighth Army was exhausted and near culmination. Macarthur's inability to transition quickly and smoothly caused a critical loss of momentum for the U.N. attack and missed an important opportunity to employ X Corps to pressure the weakened NKPA. Even in the absence of CCF intervention, the plan for the offensive in the north was not optimal.

Operations in North Korea did little to leverage a position of relative advantage while linking tactical actions to reach a strategic objective. The basic tactical actions of MacArthur's plan appear sound. MacArthur planned for Eighth Army to seize Pyongyang, while X Corps secured Wonsan Harbor and then link-up with Eight Army along the Wonsan-Pyongyang corridor to trap fleeing NKPA. However, late in October, MacArthur directed Eighth Army forces and ROK elements of X Corps to advance as rapidly as possible toward the Manchurian border.[106] This terrain-focused directive did little to hasten the defeat of the NKPA. Additionally it put U.N. forces in a disadvantageous position. As forces moved north, the peninsula becomes wider, resulting in wide dispersion of divisions.[107] The plan described above, with forces arrayed to defeat a weak and demoralized NKPA, did not posture U.N. forces to

---

[104] Milkowski, "After Inchon," in *On Operational Art,* 422.

[105] James, *The Years of MacArthur: Triumph and Disaster 1945-1964,* 493.

[106] *Ibid.,* 499.

[107] *Ibid.,* 532.

counter a massive CCF assault. What was missing in MacArthur's directive was a plan that leveraged the U.N. strength in firepower and with forces postured for mutual support.

The plan to invade North Korea demonstrated little understanding of the potential change in the operational environment resulting from CCF intervention, hastily changed strategic objectives, and transition to operations in North Korea. Two major shifts in the operating environment affected operations in this phase. First, the addition of a new enemy, the CCF, after fighting for months and sent north with limited supplies approached its culminating point.

As he ordered the attack into North Korea, MacArthur was unaware of the CCF intentions or capabilities. MacArthur should have anticipated the nature of the developing battlefield further in advance and with greater clarity. "…neither Eighth Army nor X Corps knew the size and extent of the Chinese forces in their front. They were so poorly informed and simultaneously so confident of their capability to overcome the Chinese who might oppose them, that…the U.N. expected a quick victory…"[108] MacArthur discounted the threat of the CCF to the point that realistic planning for the transition to fighting a new enemy would require. MacArthur's lapse in anticipation continued even while the CCF attacked in force. 'MacArthur, until better appraised of the situation, was pressing Walker to continue his advance."[109]

Truman and the JCS changed the strategic objective from preservation of South Korea to defeating the NPKA north of the 38th Parallel to unification the North and South only after the success of CHROMITE. A decision of this magnitude should be well thought out and comprehensively planned. Occupying all of North Korea would necessitate a colossal post war commitment of resources and personnel, but most importantly, it required plan for immediate

---

[108] Appleman, *Disaster in Korea: The Chinese Confront MacArthur,* 22.

[109] James, *The Years of MacArthur: Triumph and Disaster 1945-1964,* 527.

operations including contingency plans for Chinese or Soviet intervention. In changing the strategic objective, MacArthur neglected the later stages of CHROMITE which included defeating as much of the NKPA force in South Korea as was possible.

As operations unfolded, the ROKs secured Wonsan and Eighth Army secured Pyongyang before X Corps could complete the backload at Inchon. Additionally the North Koreans mined the harbor at Wonsan with over 3000 floating mines.[110] Although the Navy would need to clear Wonsan port eventually, the urgent need to need to conduct the amphibious assault using X Corps was no longer necessary sine the ROKA secured some three weeks earlier. Had MacArthur obtained a better understanding of the operational environment he could have avoided the confusion of unnecessary movements, loss in momentum, and logistics shortfalls caused by tying up critical assets. As the operational environment unfolded, adaptations that could provide a better employment of the force were not considered.

During this phase, MacArthur did not seek to expand and refine understanding of the operational environment. The lack of understanding of the operational environment in this phase is confounding, especially considering MacArthur's brilliant vision and execution up to this point. Although a matter of strategic importance, MacArthur failed to adequately anticipate the operational impact of CCF intervention and the limits of air power to secure the border. After the Success of Inchon, his superiors hesitated to question his judgment when pushing North to the Yalu " despite all evidence that prophesized disaster."[111] When the plan began to unravel, he did little with the force he had to prevent it. He believed the CCF had the capability to force U.N. forces out of Korea, despite the military advantages the U.N. possessed. He made recommendations to the president and JCS to expand the war to China, which was fundamentally

---

[110] Cagle and Manson, *The Sea War in Korea*, 146-147.

[111] George C. Mitchell, *Matthew B. Ridgway: Soldier, Statesman, Scholar, Citizen* (Mechanicsburg, PA: Stackpole Books 2002), 92.

not in line with policy. In a 6 December, MacArthur informed the Army Chief of Staff "If the existing restrictions on his forces were continued and no reinforcements were forthcoming, [he] believed the UNC forces should be evacuated to avoid their destruction. If Red China were subjected to naval blockade and bombing and nationalist reinforcements were approved his forces could hold in Korea."[112] This recommendation to expand the war or evacuate, and the optimism that air power alone could isolate the Korean peninsula demonstrates that that MacArthur did little to expand his understanding of the operational environment in this phase of the war. By February 1951, MacArthur's drastic assessment of the situation and the measures that the U.N. should take were proved categorically wrong as early as January 1951.[113]

During this period, MacArthur displayed an inability to avoid the constraint of preconceived notions of solutions. Macarthur and his subordinates discounted intelligence on CCF intentions despite the multitude of intelligence pointing to the CCF entrance into the war. Later Ridgway assessed that MacArthur had an "overriding belief he was right closed his mind to all counsel. It simply cannot be argued that MacArthur was unaware of the enemy's presence or his capabilities."[114] Later when CCF intervention could no longer be ignored, MacArthur's only planned reaction, isolation of the battlefield with airpower, was also flawed. U.N. forces may have been able to defeat the CCF attacks in North Korea with proper analysis and effective counter measures. He also failed to amend his plan for fighting with X Corps separately, even when the ROKA secured Wonsan before X corps finished back loading at Inchon. The plan, designed with the preconceived notion that CCF intervention was unlikely "was perfectly suited to the pursuit and destruction of a weakened [NKPA] whose remnant forces were fugitive deep in

---

[112] James, *The Years of MacArthur: Triumph and Disaster 1945-1964*, 538.

[113] Schnabel, *The United States Army and the Korean War Policy and Direction: The First Year*, 38. "Although the measures [MacArthur] had recommended against the Chinese outside of Korea had not been taken and no reinforcements had arrived, MacArthur's command had not been driven out of Korea."

[114] Mitchell, *Matthew B. Ridgway: Soldier, Statesman, Scholar, Citizen*, 92.

North Korea."[115] Even after the first CCF attack in late October checked Eighth Army's advance, MacArthur failed to alter his preconceived notion of Chinese intentions or the possibility that his forces were committed past the point of culmination. Instead, he ordered all forces to continue the "drive forward to the Yalu as rapidly as possible with all forces under their command."[116]

Overall, the operational leadership of MacArthur in this phase failed to adequately meet the requirements of operational art in every category and resulted in a military defeat. After the withdrawal of U.N. Forces back south of the 38th Parallel, the strategic aim of the U.N eventually reverted back to an armistice and status quo ante. [117]

Case Three: U.N. Counteroffensive, 25 January - 8 July 1951

The transition of the operational initiative from the CCF to the U.N. forces in January 1951 also marked the transition to a separate phase of the Korean War. In this phase, Ridgway radically retooled Eighth Army's fighting spirit and professionalism. Furthermore, he synchronized the operations of the entire U.N. force, enabling them to not only resume the operational initiative, but to avoid an embarrassing strategic defeat at the hands of a primitive communist force. This phase begins with the U.N. Forces in the defense south of Seoul postured to resume the offensive and regain the initiative. It ends with the U.N. forces advanced to "Line Kansas," north of the 38th parallel. This phase of the war was another excellent example of operational art in practice. In just under two months after the initial CCF attack, U.N. Forces again turned the tide of the war by wresting the initiative from the enemy and therefore denying the communists the ability to defeat the U.N. in Korea by military means alone for a second time.

---

[115] Halberstam, *The Coldest Winter: America and the Korean War*, 494.

[116] Milkowski, "After Inchon," in *On Operational Art*, 424.

[117] The term *status quo ante* is Latin, meaning literally "the state in which things were." The term used in treaties to refer to the withdrawal of enemy troops and the restoration of prewar leadership. When used as such, it means that no side gains or loses territory or economic and political rights.

Significant developments occurred in the midst of the Chinese intervention and U.N. withdrawal from North Korea. By early January, the communist occupied territory south of the 38th parallel and recaptured Seoul. "In just two months, the Chinese changed the conflict's strategic context."[118] U.N. forces withdrew to a defensive line south of the Han River. China's official entrance into the war caused the U.N. and the United States to abandon its short-term aim of unifying the two Koreas. The ambiguity of the strategic aim of the U.N. slowly solidified to preservation of the Republic of South Korea with the two countries somewhat approximating the pre-war boundaries at the 38th parallel or status quo ante.[119]

In another critical development, a jeep accident in late December 1950 killed the Eighth Army Commander, General Walker. General Matthew Ridgway "assumed command of a defeated, retreating, and broken Eighth Army."[120] Ridgway, a distinguished airborne general, set out immediately to stabilize the crisis in Korea and set the conditions for an immediate offensive. Latitude was not a privilege MacArthur extended to Almond or Walker. However, in the operational aftershock of the fiasco in North Korea, MacArthur allowed Ridgway maximum latitude to carry out operations, in effect making him the most prominent operational commander in this case study.

Starting on 25 January 1951, Ridgway's Eighth Army, now with X Corps consolidated under its command, pushed northward in a sharp series of carefully planned offensives aimed at advancing to defensible terrain.[121] By late April, Eighth Army recaptured almost all of South

---

[118] Millett, *The War for Korea,1950-1951: They Came From the North,* 291.

[119] Billy C. Mossman, *Ebb and Flow, November 1950-July 1951: United States Army in the Korean War* (Washington, D.C. : Department of the Army, Chief of Military History 1988), 490. Although a general understanding existed to the shift in the strategic aim, the JCS did not officially direct Ridgway to seek a negotiated settlement until 1 June 1951.

[120] Adrian R. Lewis, *The American Culture of War: A History of US Military Force from World War II to Operation Enduring Freedom*, 2 ed. (New York: Routledge, 2012), 109.

[121] Operations conducted in this Phase:

Korea and occupied a defensive line generally well above the 38th Parallel. In mid-May, the CCF attempted a massive counter offensive, gaining ground across the peninsula, but at such great expense that U.N. forces quickly recovered their losses and advanced further into North Korean territory. The U.N. operational offensive ended in June of 1951. U.N. forces reverted to an operational defense on the Kansas-Wyoming Line near the Iron Triangle.[122] The front remained relatively static for much of the rest of the war. Further gains in North Korean territory were militarily unnecessary to negotiate for the *status quo ante*.

In April, Truman relieved MacArthur as Commander of the United Nations Forces. Despite several warnings from Truman, MacArthur has repeatedly made public statements, which conflicted with the President's policy in Korea and Taiwan.[123] Truman replaced MacArthur with Ridgway and General James Van Fleet replaced Ridgway as commander of the U.S. Eighth Army.

Ridgway's approach in this phase of the conflict correctly balanced risk and opportunity. With China now in the war, "the Korean problem would not be solved by military action alone."[124] Military operations had to strike a balance of retaining the initiative but remain restrained in order to reduce the risk of escalation. Total annihilation of a communist opponent

---

OPERATION THUNDERBOLT - Armed reconnaissance to retake offensive 25 Jan-20 Feb 1951;

OPERATION KILLER – Attack to reestablish U.N. Line east of Wonju 21 Feb-7 March 1951;

OPERATION RIPPER – Attack to outflank Seoul and capture Chunchon 7 March-4 April 1951;

OPERATION RUGGED - Attack secure Phase Line Kansas n. of 38th parallel 1-15 April 1951; and

OPERATION DAUNTLESS - Attack secure Phase Line Utah forward to Line Kansas 10-22 April 1951

[122] The Iron Triangle is an area located 20 to 30 miles above the 38th parallel in the center of the peninsula south of Pyongyang. It served as a key communist assembly area and communications junction. It contained the major road and rail links between the port of Wonsan in the northeast and Seoul in the southwest.

[123] Pearlman, *Truman & MacArthur: Policy, Politics, and the Hunger For Honor and Renown*, 192-195.

[124] Schnabel, *The United States Army and the Korean War Policy and Direction: The First Year*, 384.

was excessively dangerous. The JCS directed purpose of Ridgway's operations was to "create conditions favorable to the settlement of the Korean conflict."[125] Clausewitz phrased this purpose similarly: "The end is either to bring the enemy to his knees or at least deprive him of some of his territory–the point in that case being not to improve the current military position but to improve one's general prospects in the war and in peace negotiations."[126] In Ridgway's case, U.N. actions now had to overcome the will of the enemy without eliminating his capability to resist. Ridgway's approach, similar to General Winfield Scott's Mexico City campaign in 1847, was the deliberate and inevitable advance of his army.[127] The aim of this approach was to erode the will of the enemy by demonstrating the futility in resistance. Ridgway now viewed his operational objective as inflicting heavy casualties on the enemy without risking his force unnecessarily. Ridgway's job, in other words, was "to make the Chinese pay so high a price that victory would seem out of reach."[128] He decided the war "was no longer going to be primarily about gaining terrain as an end in itself, but about selecting the most advantageous positions available, making a stand, and bleeding enemy forces, inflicting maximum casualties on them."[129] He limited risk by advancing beyond the 38th parallel only as far as justified by military necessity to bring them to the bargaining table. Using this approach, Ridgway skillfully managed transitions between offense and defense to balance operational risk to his force while at the same time retaining the initiative to exploit the opportunity to deplete the enemy's combat power and political endurance.

---

[125] *Ibid.,* 396.

[126] Clausewitz, *On War*, 570.

[127] The flaw in this comparison is that in June of 1951, The U.N. stopped advancing for various reasons of policy. The result is that the CCF felt no pressure to conclude an armistice and the Korean War continued into 1953.

[128] Halberstam, *The Coldest Winter: America and the Korean War*, 495.

[129] *Ibid.,* 501.

Ridgway was committed to return to the offensive just as quickly as Eighth Army's strength permitted. **He immediately created and maintained the conditions necessary to seize, retain, and exploit the initiative.** Before he could recapture the initiative, he first had to restore the fighting spirit and confidence of Eighth Army. Ridgway noted, "Before going on the offensive, we had work to do, weaknesses to shore up, mistakes to learn from, faulty procedures to correct, and a sense of pride to restore."[130]

When the CCF mauled U.N. forces in North Korea, Eighth Army suffered tremendous casualties and loss of equipment, but the far greater damage was "the resulting defeat had crushed [Eighth Army's] morale."[131] While Ridgway believed the Eighth Army had the strength and means to defeat the enemy "most of his commanders did not share his confidence."[132] His dominant problem was "to achieve the spiritual awakening of the latent capabilities of this command." If he could manage this, he was certain that the Eighth Army would "achieve more, far more, than our people think possible-and perhaps inflict a bloody defeat on the Chinese which even China will long remember."[133] Ridgway immediately initiated actions to improve the welfare and morale of soldiers, to retrain them, and to restore their fighting spirit. He directed his leaders to provide their soldiers everything they needed to fight in the harsh Korean winter, to include hot meals and warm clothing. Additionally, Ridgway reinforced to soldiers the purpose of the war by telling them why they were fighting in Korea.

To generate enough combat power to seize retain and exploit the initiative, Ridgway directed adjustments to the tactical employment of Eighth Army to match his operational

---

[130] Ridgway, *The Korean War*, 97.

[131] Halberstam, *The Coldest Winter: America and the Korean War*, 497.

[132] Mossman, *Ebb and Flow, November 1950-July 1951: United States Army in the Korean War*, 209.

[133] *Ibid.*, 209.

approach. He believed Eighth Army was not fighting has effectively as it should against an inferior CCF. He had "found only one or two cases where a Division has shown any appreciable resourcefulness in adapting its fighting tactics to the terrain, to the enemy, and to conditions in this theater."[134] In Ridgway's appraisal, the Eighth Army was "...opposed by an enemy whose only advantage is sheer numbers, whose armament is far inferior quantitatively and qualitatively, who has no air support whatsoever, meager telecommunications and negligible armor."[135]

On his initial tour of the front, he gathered his corps commanders and issued simple standing orders guiding U.N. actions and tactics.[136] He directed immediate improvements in leadership presence on the front lines, increased reconnaissance and patrolling, and mandated immediate training in night fighting and marches. He mandated maintaining mutual support with adjacent units in all operations. Additionally he directed improvements in the planning and employment of one of the U.N. key combat advantages specifically tailored to defeat he numerically superior enemy – massive artillery firepower.[137] Results of these changes were instantly evident in the improved the combat proficiency of Eighth Army.

In this phase of the Korean War, Ridgway achieved a position of relative advantage by clearly linked tactical actions to reach a strategic objective. His efforts to improve the morale and fighting spirit of Eighth army were the first step in gaining a position of relative advantage and stopping the communist advance south. Next Ridgway stabilized his position south of the Han River in defensible terrain. He requested additional artillery divisions and Korean

---

[134] *Ibid.*, 210.

[135] *Ibid.*, 209.

[136] Blair, *The Forgotten War: America in Korea, 1950-1953*, 586-587.

[137] *Ibid.*, 586. Ridgway noted that infantry units typically used less than a third of their artillery fire provided to them, yet routinely requested other means of support and reinforcement. In Ridgway's view, using artillery effectively not only contributed to his purpose of attrition of the CCF, it also limited risk of CCF penetration.

laborers to help move supplies and prepare positions. Not wanting to stay in a static defense, he transitioned operations to a "limited offensive-defensive posture" aimed at establishing contact with the enemy and assess his disposition and strength.[138] When he found the CCF had limited presence to his front, he conducted reconnaissance in force operations to secure forward positions. This methodical approach not only enabled Ridgway to recover Korean terrain, it established continuous contact with the enemy and allowed Ridgway to set the tempo of operations.

Ridgway's overall offensive plan was to advance and occupy a series of phase lines running laterally across the peninsula along defensible terrain. Throughout the spring of 1951, these phase lines served as successive operational objectives to advance the forward line of troops north. To Ridgway, movement was less important than attrition of the enemy. Ridgway's offensives, intended to kill Communist troops with no particular territorial gains in mind, had the opposite effect. The CCF "for the most part pulled back intact before the U.N. offenses, but in doing so gave up substantial territory. It was the Communist offensives that killed off so many of their troops."[139] Before Ridgway's directions, U.N. forces, would withdraw to avoid anticipated encirclement when attacked in strength. "Ridgway realized it was a disaster to retreat once the Chinese hit" and instead encouraged U.N. units stand and fight.[140] He disciplined leaders who withdrew "without evidence of having inflicted any substantial losses on the enemy."[141] Major engagements in February 1951 such as Wonju and Chip'yong-ni signaled a change in U.S. battlefield tactics and demonstrated the effectiveness of Eighth Army's tactical improvements.

---

[138] *Ibid.*, 571.

[139] Stanley Sandler, *The Korean War: An Interpretative History* (London: Routledge, 1999), 67.

[140] Halberstam, *The Coldest Winter: America and the Korean War*, 501.

[141] Mossman, *Ebb and Flow, November 1950-July 1951: United States Army in the Korean War*, 216.

U.N Forces backed by artillery and air, stood and fought against massive CCF assaults. Stopping the CCF offenses demonstrated Eighth Army substantially regained the confidence and spirit it lost during the long retreat from North Korea. His guidance for Eighth Army to maintain contact and fight enabled his tactical actions to serve the operational objective of inflicting heavy casualties on the enemy.

Ridgway understood the operational environment, the strategic objectives, and the capabilities of all elements of his force. Before arriving in Korea, Ridgway had a unique perspective of the complexities of the Korean War. Ridgway assumed command in Korea directly from his previous assignment as Deputy Chief of Staff for the Army, where he monitored the events of the war daily. He also was aware of the Pentagon views of how to prosecute the war. Ridgway had served with MacArthur as his aide and was aware "just how shrewdly MacArthur rationed the truth."[142] This outside perspective enabled Ridgway to form an independent opinion and a plan on how to win in Korea.

The JCS informed Ridgway that he could not expect further reinforcements. Consequently, Ridgway had to exercise his tactical options conservatively to limit the risk to his force. Ridgway explained his concept for operations as "inflict maximum damage on the enemy with minimum [on U.N. Forces], the maintaining of all major units in fact, a careful avoidance of being sucked into a trap – by ruse or as a result of our own aggressiveness – to be destroyed piecemeal. We will pursue only to a point where we are able to provide powerful support."[143] He limited operational maneuver to a series of well-planned phase lines. Aided by thorough reconnaissance and patrolling, he advanced his front only to occupy defensible terrain and to

---

[142] Halberstam, *The Coldest Winter: America and the Korean War,* 102.

[143] Ridgway, *The Korean War,* 108.

maintain continuous contact with the CCF. By doing this, he avoided the risk of pursuing objectives that were beyond his force's capability to reinforce or defend.

Ridgway took steps to continually expand and refine understanding of the operational environment. He focused intelligence efforts to develop an understanding of the CCF tactics and even the capabilities of its units and commanders. He routinely traveled from unit to unit meeting with commanders. For a time he "started his day flying in a small plane…looking for enemy."[144] He used the knowledge he acquired about the enemy to play at least as big a role in the selection of the battlefield as his Chinese opposites."[145] His ability to learn from the enemy was the marked difference from his predecessors. In effort to offset gaps in intelligence, he immediately ordered vigorous patrolling to establish and maintain contact with the enemy. Ridgway saw the main mission of vigorous patrolling was "to acquire better combat intelligence, which in his judgment had been sadly neglected and which was a prime requisite for the still larger offensive action that he intended would follow."[146] Patrolling revealed the enemy position and strength, permitting Ridgway to "obtain an accurate picture of the enemy's power and deployment." Although the lack of reliable intelligence was of concern to Ridgway, he did not allow it to deter the offensive operations. For example, frustrated with the lack of intelligence but suspecting the enemy lightly defended the area south of the Han River, Ridgway began Operation KILLER and immediately followed it with Operation Ripper, resulting in the eventual liberation of Seoul.

Ridgway demonstrated the ability to avoid the constraint of preconceived notions of solutions. There were several prevailing notions of solutions that did not constrain Ridgway. One

---

[144] Halberstam, *The Coldest Winter: America and the Korean War*, 500.

[145] *Ibid.*, 502.

[146] Mossman, *Ebb and Flow, November 1950-July 1951: United States Army in the Korean War*, 216.

such notion was that victory in Korea required a decisive military defeat of the enemy. Ridgway strictly aligned his operations to the strategy objective– the limited objective of forcing the enemy to negotiations table. Ridgway understood that gradual and deliberate attrition would defeat the communists on the battlefield and enforce the U.N. bargaining position while not escalating the conflict. Another preconceived notion, promoted by MacArthur, was that unless heavily reinforced, the U.N. could not win against the numerically superior CCF. When Ridgway took command of a defeated Eighth Army, the prevailing attitude was that the U.S. should withdraw from Korea as quickly as possible.[147] Ridgway smashed such notions when he stopped the CCF offensive and south of Seoul and immediately began an effective advance back to the 38th Parallel. Ridgway was almost alone in thinking the dire situation in Korea was reversible.

The third notion was that Eight Army was beaten and helpless against the CCF. He did not believe this and to counter it, he focused on rebuilding the fighting spirit of the demoralized Eighth Army. Ridgway changed leadership when he saw that his subordinates, including regimental, division, and corps commanders, could not or would not execute his orders. His immediate efforts to improve sustainment to Eighth Army and medical capability to improved fighting spirit and morale. He modified the tactics used by his Eighth Army from one of constant retreat and limited contact with the CCF to maintaining constant pressure on their forces designed to cause as much destruction to the enemy force as possible. Realizing a vulnerability of the enemy was his susceptibility to culminate relatively early after an offensive, he exploited the opportunity to counter attack after CCF major offensives, ensuring Eight Army focused on inflicting casualties.

Ridgway's campaign demonstrates an effective application of the six requirements of operational art. After completing a successful withdrawal and defense, Ridgway's Army mounted

---

[147] Appleman, *Ridgway Duels for Korea*, 665.

a series of offensive operations to regain lost territory and reestablish the defensive line along the 38th Parallel. Ridgway, as the operational commander, successfully wrested the initiative back from the enemy. During the period of Ridgway's command, from late December of 1950 through April of 1951, the Eighth Army stopped a major offensive campaign conducted by the CCF. He set the stage for Van Fleet's assumption of command of eighth army and continued his stewardship of the war as Commander of U.N. forces. The success of this phase within the guidelines of policy is undeniable. Thus, this case study illustrates the importance of operational arts requirements

Conclusion

The Korean War serves as an example of how both strategy and policy strategy can evolve during the course conflict and how the conduct of operations must adapt to meet strategy requirements. Both the success and failures of the operational commanders in the Korean War serve equally as examples of the value of operational art. The three phases of the Korean War presented above, illustrate the validity of the requirements of operational art as framework for a successful campaign. The Korean War, particularly with the changing nature the first year, provides an excellent subject for operational art study. Analyzing operational art requirements in relation to the operational actions of the Korean War provide an example of how the success or failure is determined by the commander's ability to link tactical actions in time, space, and purpose in pursuit of a strategic objective.

The conditions that cause the Korean War began long before June 1951. The US and the U.N. fought in Korea to protect vital interests larger than Korea itself. American shortsightedness in recognizing the strategic importance of Korea after World War II and the intentions of the USSR and China to build an offense of capable North Korea contributed to the strategic context of the conflict. In the beginning of the war, the method of prosecution of the conflict was easy to determine. MacArthur needed to build up enough combat power to seize the initiative, when the offensive has taken back the initiative, seek a decisive victory through military means. During the first three months of the war, MacArthur designed and executed a brilliant campaign in a seemingly textbook example of operational art. However, MacArthur disregarded prudence and the concepts at the core foundation of operational when he recklessly attacked into North Korea. When the Chinese entered the war in the second phase, military means were not enough to reach the strategic objective within the price the political leaders were willing to pay. Ridgway had to adjust his operational approach to completely new strategic problem. MacArthur was not willing to adjust what he believed was the outcome of victory in Asia, and so he was relieved of his command. Ridgway, understanding the strategic purpose of the war as containing communist aggression without expanding the war, limited his operations and focused on defeating the CCF inside of Korea. Ridgway's knowledge of his mission and employment of his force fulfilled all six requirements of operational art.

Finally, the requirements of operational art, as stated in ADP 3-0 are crucial guidelines in designing a cohesive campaign. Although not codified in doctrine at the time of the Korean War, operational concepts remain unchanged in modern warfare. An analysis of the Korean War shows when operational art concepts were taken into account for the purposes of designing and executing the campaign, and when they were not. The instances also correlate to success and failure, demonstrating the validity of operational art in today's theory and doctrine.

BIBLIOGRAPHY

Alexander, Bevin. *Korea: The First War We Lost*. New York: Hippocrene, 1986.

Appleman, Roy Edgar. *South to the Naktong, North to the Yalu*. United States Army in the Korean War. Washington, D.C. : Department of the Army, Chief of Military History: 1961.

————. *Escaping the Trap: The US Army X Corps in Northeast Korea, 1950*. College Station, TX: Texas A & M University Press, 1990.

————. *Disaster in Korea: The Chinese Confront MacArthur*. College Station, TX: Texas A & M University Press, 1989.

————. *East of Chosin: Entrapment and Breakout in Korea, 1950*. College Station, TX: Texas A&M University Press, 1987.

————. *Ridgway Duels for Korea*. Texas A&M University Military History Series. College Station, TX: Texas A&M University Press, 1990.

Bartlett, Merrill L. *Assault from the Sea: Essays on the History of Amphibious Warfare*. Annapolis, MD.: Naval Institute Press, 1983.

Blair, Clay. *The Forgotten War: America in Korea, 1950-1953*. New York: Anchor Books, 1989.

Cagle, Malcolm W. and Frank Albert Manson. *The Sea War in Korea*. Annapolis, MD: United States Naval Institute, 1957.

Catchpole, Brian. *The Korean War, 1950-53*. New York: Carroll & Graf Publishers, 2000.

Clausewitz, Carl Von, *On War* edited by Michael Eliot Howard, and Peter Paret. Princeton, N.J.: Princeton University Press, 1984.

Futrell, Robert Frank. *The United States Air Force in Korea, 1950-1953*. New York: Duell, Sloan and Pearce, 1961.

Goulden, Joseph C. *Korea : The Untold Story of the War*. New York: Times Books, 1982.

Halberstam, David. *The Coldest Winter: America and the Korean War*. New York: Hyperion, 2007.

Hamburger, Kenneth E. *Leadership in the Crucible: the Korean War Battles of Twin Tunnels & Chipyong-Ni*. College Station,TX: Texas A&M University Press, 2003.

Hastings, Max. *The Korean War*. New York: Simon and Schuster, 1987.

Hoyt, Edwin Palmer. *On to the Yalu*. New York: Stein and Day, 1985.

James, D. Clayton. *The Years of Macarthur: Triumph and Disaster 1945-1964*. Vol. 3.Boston: Houghton Mifflin, 1985.

Kissinger, Henry. *Diplomacy*. New York: Simon & Schuster, 1994.

Krause, Michael D., R. Cody Phillips, and Center of Military History. *Historical Perspectives of the Operational Art*. Washington, D.C.: Center of Military History, United States Army, 2005.

Lowe, Peter. *The Origins of the Korean War*. New York: Longman, 1997.

Lewis, Adrian R. *The American Culture of War: A History of US Military Force from World War II to Operation Enduring Freedom*, 2 ed. NewYork: Routledge, 2012.

MacDonald, Callum A. *Korea, the War Before Vietnam.* New York: Free Press, 1987.

Millett, Allan R. *The War For Korea, 1945-1950: A House Burning.* Lawrence, KS: University Press of Kansas, 2005.

Millett, Allan Reed. *The War for Korea,1950-1951: They Came From the North.* Lawrence, KS: University Press of Kansas, 2005.

Mintzberg, Henry. *The Rise and Fall of Strategic Planning: Reconceiving Roles for Planning, Plans, Planners.* New York: Free Press, 1994.

Momyer, William W. *Airpower in Three Wars.* Maxwell Air Force Base, AL: Air University Press, 2003.

Mossman, Billy C. *Ebb and Flow, November 1950-July 1951, United States Army in the Korean War.* Washington, D.C. : Department of the Army, Chief of Military History, 1988.

Mitchell, George C. *Matthew B. Ridgway: Soldier, Statesman, Scholar, Citizen.* Mechanicsburg, PA: Stackpole Books, 2002.

Pearlman, Michael D. *Truman & MacArthur: Policy, Politics, and the Hunger for Honor and Renown.* Bloomington: Indiana University Press, 2008.

Rees, David. *Korea: The Limited War.* Baltimore: Penguin Books, 1970.

Ridgway, Matthew B. *The Korean War.* Garden City, New York: Doubleday, 1967.

Sandler, Stanley. *The Korean War: An Interpretative History.* London: Routledge, 1999.

Schnabel, James F. *The United States Army and the Korean War Policy and Direction: The First Year.* Washington D.C.: U.S. Army Center of Military History, 1992.

Smith, Robert. *MacArthur in Korea: The Naked Emperor.* New York: Simon and Schuster, 1982.

Stokesbury, James L. *A Short History of the Korean War.* New York: W. Morrow, 1988.

Stueck, William Whitney. *Rethinking the Korean War: A New Diplomatic and Strategic History.* Princeton, N.J.: Princeton University Press, 2002.

Stueck, William, *The Korean War in World History.* Lexington, KY: The University Press of Kentucky, 2004.

Summers, Harry G. *Korean War Almanac.* New York: Facts on File, 1990.

Swain, Richard M. *Filling the Void: The Operational Art and the U.S. Army.* Fort Leavenworth, KS: U.S. Army Command and General Staff College, 1992.

Toland, John. *In Mortal Combat: Korea, 1950-1953.* New York: Morrow, 1996.

U.S. Department of the Army. *FM 1-02 2004: Operational Terms and Graphics.* Washington, D.C.: U.S. Department of the Army, 2004.

_____. *FM 3-0: Operations* (Change 1, 28 Feb 2011). Washington, D.C.: U.S. Department of the Army, 2009.

Vego, Milan. "Military History and the Study of Operational Art." *JFQ: Joint Force Quarterly,* no. 57 (2010): 124-9.

Weintraub, Stanley. *MacArthur's War: Korea and the Undoing of an American Hero.* New York: Free Press, 2000.

www.ingramcontent.com/pod-product-compliance
Lightning Source LLC
Chambersburg PA
CBHW080611290526
45790CB00007B/2727